Miracle of Minden

written by Krystal D. Greer

A TRUE STORY

Miracle of Minden

is dedicated to all of my children.

All of you are miracles.

Table of Contents

Introduction

My name is Krystal Greer, and I am the daughter of Rev. & Mrs. Bill R. Mills. When Dad approached me about writing *Miracle of Minden*, I remember telling him right away that the only way I could share this story was from my point of view. I cannot share his story from his perspective. Dad's gracious reply to me that day was, "Because you are part of my story, you can tell it in your own words." He told me he tried to write down his miracle, but the words simply would not come. While Dad is a divinely anointed speaker, he does not particularly enjoy writing. His natural medium of communication is the spoken word. I have worked for

Dad at several points in my life and making heads or tails of his notes was almost impossible at times. Writing is simply not his forté. Yet, Dad believed *Miracle of Minden* must be written and he chose me to write it.

I am honored to share this story with you. As the daughter of an evangelist, I possess unique experience with miracles. The earliest miracle I can remember must have happened when I was around ten years old.

My dad was preaching a tent revival in Denton, Texas in the heat of summer. Aside from the miracle that occurred under that tent, all I remember is the heat. One night, no different in my mind from any other night, a family with a young light-haired boy went to the altar. During my research for this project, I found out the names of this family from one of the newspaper articles written for Denton Record Chronicle by Ms. Stephanie McCollum and photographed by Mr. Allan Key. Donna and Robert McCauley brought their three-year-old son, Shane, to the tent revival that night.

I saw men of God lay their hands on that baby and pray for him. The next thing I saw was the boy covering his ears with his hands. It dawned on me that the toddler could hear! Shane was deaf and the first thing he heard was an excited, passionate Pentecostal preacher praying for him!

The entire congregation exploded in worship and praise. The boy looked scared to death, but he could hear! I do not remember all the details of this miracle, but the life of one young soul was forever changed that night.

What a difference a day makes! When Donna McCauley woke up that morning, did she have any idea that her son would be able to hear when he went to bed that night? What drew her to that tent revival that night? Was she desperate to get help for her child? Maybe she just wanted to see what all the fuss was about. Everybody in town was talking about this tent revival, so something big must be happening with those Pentecostal folks! Whatever the reason, she brought her son to the tent revival that night with no hearing. When they left, he could hear perfectly. That was the first miracle I ever witnessed!

Throughout my childhood, we saw many miracles of healing and deliverance while travelling the United States. Dad faithfully preached the Word and souls were filled with the Holy Ghost across the land. Sharing all the miracles experienced during our travels would take much more skill than I possess, but there are a few more miracles dear to my heart you need to know in order to understand my unique experience with miracles.

When my son, Kye, was about eighteen months old, my Dad was preaching at Apostolic Faith Chapel in Gilbert, Louisiana for Brother Virgil (Bo) Harris. Kye was playing at the end of my pew and I told him to come sit down. He just ignored me, so I exited the pew where he was playing. I picked him up and carried him to the nursery where I proceeded to fuss a bit. Kye leaned his head back and stopped breathing. I heard his breath catch and then stop. My child was not breathing.

I was eighteen and I had absolutely no idea what to do to make him breathe. I ran out of the nursery to my mother screaming, "He is not breathing!" She saw he was not breathing and feebly attempted to help him. Then, she went running to Dad and almost threw my baby at him when she saw Kye's lips were turning blue. Dad turned Kye upside down and patted his back. Nothing happened. My baby was dying before my eyes.

Everyone in the building was praying for God to intervene. A nurse was up at the front with Dad trying to help. Suddenly, Dad stuck his finger down Kye's throat, (which is certainly not protocol) and when he did, Kye caught his breath and started quietly crying. Everyone says never to stick your finger down someone's throat if they are choking because you may cause further damage.

Kye had not been eating and Dad said he felt nothing in Kye's throat. I played the moment in the nursery over and over in my mind. Kye leaned his head back. I heard his breath catch and stop. Dad later said he just felt like he absolutely had to do it to save Kye's life. When Kye began to breathe, it dawned on me that we were many miles away from the nearest hospital. If Dad had not acted, Kye would have never made it anywhere to get help. My Kye is a miracle.

This miracle left me with scars. I was alone with my baby and he quit breathing. Since that day, I have rarely been alone with a child as it scares me to death. To be responsible for a life, knowing how fragile life is, immensely intimidates me. In January of 1999, I gave birth to a beautiful baby girl in New Orleans, Louisiana.

Knowing that this baby needed much more than I could ever possibly give her, I prayed and prayed. 'Answered Prayer Adoptions' handled the adoption of my baby girl. The day I signed those adoption papers began a lifelong prayer to know my baby someday. I wanted her and loved her so much. At the same time, I wanted her to have a chance in life. With me, I knew she would have none.

In March of 2017, my daughter, Jade, contacted me! I absolutely had no right to have a relationship with her, but

God made a way! I consistently laid my child on the altar in prayer. I prayed for her every time I prayed. I longed for her physically. I longed to see her, to touch her, and to know her.

On Mother's Day and her birthday every year, I literally fell apart. Then God showed up and gave me yet another miracle. God gave me Jade. I know her. She knows me. I met her in April of 2017. Since then, we have shared several visits, each more precious than the last. I get to know more and more of this amazing woman who is an answer to prayers. She was an answer to her adopted parents' prayers and now she is an answer to my earnest prayers.

I am no stranger to miracles. Since I was a child, the miraculous has been a part of my life. Any one of these few miracles I just shared with you could be expanded into a project of its own along with a plethora of other 'miracles, signs, and wonders that follow them that believe' experienced by my family. While all these miracles are part of the rich tapestry of my past, they are not the *Miracle of Minden*. No, Dad's miracle is all his own. I wish I were a good enough writer to give you his story in his words, but I cannot. I hope that *Miracle of Minden* will bless you. I pray when you finish reading my account of these events, you will know beyond a shadow of a doubt that miracles are real.

Strawberries

I work for a non-profit organization that provides services for the disabled. I work at the corporate office of Evergreen Life Services, billing Medicaid in three different states, and I absolutely love my job. This is the first time in my entire life I can say that I love my job and totally mean it. I had a few other jobs that I enjoyed, but I am deeply passionate about this job.

I struggle with mental health issues that on many occasions in my past prevented me from finding joy and satisfaction in my work. All that changed the day I walked through the door God opened specifically for me at Evergreen Life Services. I have a Bachelor of Arts degree in English and have never taken a single class in accounting. I had absolutely no experience or qualifications for this position, but my interviewer took a chance on me and forever changed my life! I found favor and grace with this organization, and I was promoted quickly. Most days, I leave my office feeling blessed and fulfilled. Please understand I do not have a perfect job. No one does. That is why they call it work instead of play. Jobs are simply hard. However, I feel valued and I know the work I do makes possible all the services provided for the disabled individuals served by the organization.

The largest fundraiser for the small congregation at Apostolic Lighthouse of Minden, Louisiana is selling chocolate covered strawberries for Valentine's Day. The ladies' department has sponsored this fundraiser for many years. If you have ever worked in Medicaid billing, you know that it is a big cycle. Working in multiple states means the month must be carefully planned to ensure all deadlines are met so that the claims are paid on time. As a non-profit organization, the money must be received timely to ensure payroll is met and bills are paid. Billing is what makes the wheel go around, so to speak. Because February is a short month, the timing in February is extremely critical. Due to my hectic work schedule in February, my normal contribution to this fundraiser is to buy and sell as many strawberries as possible. I never felt like it was possible for me to take a vacation day and work at the church with everyone. This day begins at 3:00 a.m. and usually wraps up around 3:00 p.m. The ladies have dipped up to three hundred dozen strawberries for delivery and pick-up on Valentine's Day.

2019 was different. Unfortunately, church attendance was down. I looked around me and saw there was a great need for me to be physically present and help with the strawberry fundraiser this year. I had to step up and do more. I prayed about it and requested the day off to work at the church with everyone.

I showed up around 8:00 a.m. that Thursday and helped in the back sprinkling the strawberries. (Have I mentioned that our strawberries are amazing? They look completely professional.) At 9:00 a.m., we open the front of the church for people to pick up strawberries previously ordered or stop in and buy on the spot. I worked the table up front and thoroughly enjoyed the interaction with the people of Minden. To me, telling people that we love them and inviting them to church is the best part of any fundraiser to me. We may be raising money, but I always take advantage of the opportunity to do some outreach also!

At the end of those long hours spent working for the Kingdom, I went to lunch with my parents before heading home to put up my tired, achy feet. After lunch, Dad went back to the church to sweep and mop all the floors and be sure that everything was ready for Sunday School. He could have waited for the work release inmates that were scheduled to volunteer at the church Saturday, but he refused to take a chance that the work would not get done. That is the kind of leader he is. He may be Pastor, but he is always first partaker in any work of the church. My parents clean the church in January and any other month that no one signs up to clean. Workdays at Apostolic Lighthouse find him sweating hard and working circles around younger men. Any time any type of work is needed for the Kingdom, Dad is the first to volunteer. Many years ago, he learned the valuable lesson that being a leader means being a servant. So, that is what he does. He serves.

I went to bed that night on Valentine's Day 2019 completely exhausted. As I drifted off to sleep, I thought about the long day working for the Kingdom and wondered if the day was a success. I wondered if we raised enough funds to send our young people to youth camp. I wondered if we sold all the strawberries so that none were wasted. I had no idea that by that time the next night, I would not care one bit about how much funds were raised from strawberries.

Friday

I love Fridays! As much as I enjoy my job, I treasure my weekends! Weekends are when I regain my sense of self. During the week, I feel like I lose part of me in the daily grind. I went to work on Friday, February 15th, 2019 thoroughly exhausted. I am not used to physical work anymore. I sit at a desk all day and work with numbers. Valentine's Day and the Strawberry fundraiser left me depleted.

I was sitting at my desk thinking about how happy I was that it was Friday. I could hardly wait to get home to begin my weekend of relaxation and recuperation! My cell phone rang, and it was Mother. She sounded a bit frustrated and told me that the police had come to her house. She said that they were air lifting Dad to LSU. I completely froze. The room was deadly silent. I shook my head and tried to form a question. In my mind, I wanted to know why Dad was in a helicopter. The words would not come out and Mother kept talking, but I had missed parts of what she said. I did catch that Dad was moving a trailer and the truck ran over him.

Again, everything seemed incredibly surreal. Time slowed to a crawl in my head. This cannot be happening. She just said Dad ran over himself with his truck. No, I missed something. I remember Mother told me to calm down and be careful driving to LSU because she did not need me to have an accident on my way. I do not remember why she said that. I was probably loud and frantic. Sometimes I do that without realizing it. The actual emotions I felt were stunned and confused. This is the struggle of social anxiety. Effectual communication is almost impossible at times.

When I stood up at my desk, suddenly I felt the room spin back into reality. Time sped up now, and I felt trembly all over. At that point, I was not exactly certain what happened, but I knew there was an emergency and I had to get to my dad. I went to my supervisor and told her what little I did know and that I needed to go to LSU. She offered to drive me over and I was grateful. I was shaky and I hate driving in Shreveport. I am blessed with an amazing supervisor. She is a miracle herself, but that is her story to tell. I will never forget her kindness to me that day. She let me talk the whole way over there. I was trying to keep from crying and looking like a loon, but she listened and chatted with me all the way there like it was no big deal at all.

When I got to the emergency room, I searched for Mother. I finally saw her through the door outside looking put together and somewhat put out. I hugged her tight. She told me that we had beat Dad to the hospital. The helicopter should be there soon. Mother did not know exactly what had happened to Dad either. She was highly aggravated that he had moved the trailer himself instead of waiting for someone to help him move it. There was no reason at all for him to move that trailer! Now what has happened to him??? None of this made any sense to either one of us. We had no idea how critical and serious his injuries were.

We saw the helicopter and rushed inside. There was a tiny private waiting room for family of trauma patients transported by air to the hospital. Some of the members of Apostolic Lighthouse soon began to arrive and wait with us. One of those who came to the Emergency Room at Oschner LSU

Health Shreveport was a young man named Gavin Hall. The Hall family has attended Apostolic Lighthouse since my Dad became the pastor there. Gavin was just a youngster when he became a part of our lives. He is an unusually motivated young man with very definite goals and aspirations in life. He works in the medical field as a paramedic and volunteers at his local fire department.

Earlier, Gavin got a call and was working with the team that was caring for a trauma patient at the Emergency Room of Minden Medical Center. In the middle of everything, he received a call from his mother which he ignored at first. When she called again, he answered gruffly as he was working and terribly busy trying to treat a head trauma that Minden Medical Center was not equipped to treat. His mother was anxious and wanted him to get to the church immediately because Pastor Mills was involved in an accident. Gavin hung up and asked who the patient was they were treating. That is when he discovered his patient was his pastor.

Dad was screaming in pain and his head was swollen and disfigured above the collar to the point Gavin did not recognize him before the call from Sister Hall, his mother. I will share more of his view of the story in an interview later in this project. Sufficed to say, Gavin was gravely concerned for the diagnosis and prognosis of my dad. He hid it well, but he knew things were bad. The question was just how bad?

I think this is when I began to realize the seriousness of what had happened to Dad. This young man grew up with my Dad. How serious were the trauma and injuries if Gavin did not recognize the face and voice of a man he knew so well?

I mean I understood right away that he was hurt but I did not know his life was in danger and no one was telling us anything. I finally realized that they did not know if he was ok or not; whether he was going to survive or not. That is why no one was telling us anything. They did not know anything. My heart kept beating funny the whole time I was sitting in this small room. On the way over to the Emergency Room, I realized I left my phone on my desk. I took this opportunity to borrow Mother's phone and went out to the hallway. I called my husband and left a message that we had a family emergency. I called my sister back because she had called me while I was still at the office. She told me to call her when I got to the hospital, and I was worried she may be trying to reach me.

While we were on the phone, I saw a doctor coming down the hall and I followed her in the small room with Karrah on the phone. We finally got a small bit of information. The doctor told us that from what she understood there was some problem with the trailer and when Dad got out to fix it the truck began rolling and pinned his shoulder and head under the wheel. (Later we found out that Dad was under the right passenger rear tire while it was spinning on his head and shoulder.) All she could tell us was that Dad was intubated and stabilized for now until they could assess the trauma by the CAT scan. My sister was able to ask intelligent questions as she works in the medical field. At that moment, I think she was the only one not panicking. Mother and I were in a state of shock and disbelief.

I do remember someone asking about his legs because that was all that we knew was hurt at that point. The doctor said his legs were fine. "His head injury is the biggest concern right now. I know little, but I knew you needed to know something. Now you know what I know." She looked very tired. She scurried away promising to bring us information just as soon as she could. I hung up the phone wishing Karrah was beside me. They decided to come up to Shreveport to be with us as we faced the unknown. I left the tiny airless waiting room and went to the bathroom to cry in peace. My insides felt like jelly. I guess I am not strong in emergencies. I try to keep my wits, but I am too emotional. Even now I still get worked up when I think about that Friday.

Friday

Part Two

I dried my tears and went out to the hall with the mindset that sooner or later we will know something, and I must wait for knowledge before I can feel any more emotions. Sometimes I can trick my silly self into compartmentalizing stuff so that I can pretend all is well while I am falling apart inside. This is what I was trying to do in the hallway of LSU that Friday afternoon. I am having a whole conversation inside my head about how to not embarrass my family while Dad is suffering somewhere in this hospital.

While I was in the hall, I saw a hospital bed being pushed my way. There were several people around the bed, and there was a foot sticking out from under the sheet. I immediately knew it was my Dad. I rushed in the room where Mother was waiting with all these people and told her that I saw Dad's foot. She immediately tried to enter the room where I told her they took him, but someone stopped her. They said we must wait, but when she asked if Dad was in there, there was no answer. I knew he was in that room, right on the other side of that door. They promised we could see him soon, and we did.

Mother and I entered the room together. I cannot describe exactly what I saw because my brain stopped for a second. I gasped for air and stopped in my tracks for a moment. Dad did not look like himself at all. He was completely unrecognizable. His entire head was swollen and bloody on the left side. He was stabilized with a neck collar of some kind and intubated, but he was entirely conscious. The room suddenly filled behind us with a ton of people wanting to see and check on Dad. I do not remember exactly who all was there during this moment, but I went to his side.

I remember telling him that Kenneth would have moved the trailer for him, and I was so deeply sorry this happened. He got agitated and started shaking his head, so I quickly hushed. Mother also asked him a couple of questions and he responded with nods or shakes. One of the people in the room prayed with Dad and we were kicked out with a swiftness. Someone came and told us where the ICU waiting room was and that Dad would be moved there until the results of all the tests came. As a herd of some kind, we all maneuvered our way to the ICU waiting room. While we were there, more friends came to be with Mother and me.

Waiting is hard and waiting is exactly what we had to do for what seemed like forever. At some point, Kenneth called me back. I asked him to come to the hospital as soon as possible. When he got there, he went to the Emergency Room. I went to find him and show him where the ICU waiting room was. About that time, Sister Donna Jo Hall and Sister Rhonda Robinson came with my phone and Subway sandwiches. I was so thankful for both. I remember thinking; 'It is probably selfish to eat Subway sandwiches when Dad is going through this, but I am hungry. I do not think being hungry will help Dad in any way. Since someone blessed us with food, I am eating!' This is the kind of ridiculous nonsense happening in my head even in the middle of an emergency.

I was thankful to have my phone so I could keep in touch with my sister. I was ready for her to be there. My mother also handed over her phone to me to keep up with all the texts and calls pouring in. Now I was manning two phones which kept me distracted and that was a blessing.

Not long after I ate my sandwich, my phone rang. My Kye was on the other end of the line. I had called him and gave him the basic information from Mother's phone when I got to the hospital. He was calling me back for more details. He called several times in a row. Once he said that he was sorry for bothering me. That pierced my heart because a phone call from my Kye has never bothered me. I love that child more than he could ever possibly know. During one of his calls, he said for me to tell his Papa that he was praying for him. That may not mean much to you, but for me this was a small miracle in and of itself. My Kye has said in the past he did not believe in God or the power of prayer. Yet, for him to humble himself and pray for his Papa's survival gave me a surge of hope and peace that carried me through the rest of that long Friday.

Later, a chaplain stopped by the ICU waiting room that afternoon. I think he came by that Friday because he received word a patient arrived at the ICU via air flight, and that is always serious. In life-or-death situations, people tend to finally turn to God. He approached us and asked if we wanted to pray. Of course, everyone with our group immediately stood up and joined hands. I think he was a bit taken back. He asked if we were all here for Mr. Mills. Everyone, except two families, was with us. Even those families joined the prayer circle. Their loved ones were also facing serious, life-threatening illnesses and they needed prayer just like Dad.

You know how Apostolics pray. People began to seek God for a miracle for the man fighting for his life in that ICU bed. In a few moments, we broke through and the Holy Ghost filled the entire waiting room. People began to speak with other tongues and rejoice in the Holy Ghost.

By the end of the prayer, we were thanking and praising God with a loud voice for the finished work of a miracle for Bill Mills. That poor chaplain did not know quite how to handle us, but I think he will always remember those folks that just about had church in the middle of a tragedy.

Soon, my sister and her husband arrived. I was so happy to see her. Being around Karrah makes me calmer. Her strength and confidence allowed me to relax. We finally got to see a doctor and we were given more information on Dad's condition. The doctor was surprised to inform us that there were no brain bleeds. She used the word 'miracle' the first time! She said because Dad takes blood thinners and aspirin daily with his heart issues and stents, it was a miracle there was no brain bleed!

His left shoulder blade was completely broken from top to bottom. From what I understand, the scapula is the hardest bone in the body to break. Dad's scapula was completely broken in two. The right shoulder had a hairline fracture. He had five broken ribs and a broken nose. The most serious injury at this point was his left orbital socket and eye. This bone was crushed, and they were concerned about the pressure on that eye causing blindness. His eye was swollen completely shut, grotesque dark purple and black hues covered the entire side of his face and top of his head.

We were each given small pink cards. This card had the visiting times for the ICU and over the next few days; this little card ran my days and nights. The doctor did allow Karrah, Mother, and me to go check on Dad for a few minutes before the schedule began. When I saw him this time, I just knew that he would survive. While I also knew this may be the hardest thing he ever had to go through, he would live and not die just like the Psalmist declared...

"I shall not die, but live, and declare the works of the LORD."
Psalm 118:17

This test would birth yet one more testimony for my Dad to declare the works of the Lord Jesus Christ.

After the last visit at the ICU Friday night, I found my car in the parking lot and I just sat there a moment. My mind was running in a million different directions. The one thought running through my mind over and over as I sat in my vehicle was 'What a difference a day makes.' Everything changed on that Friday, and I daresay nothing will ever be the same again.

Saturday

Kenneth and I went to the hospital Saturday morning for the first visit at the ICU. I was very tired; therefore, the day is a bit of a blur. Hospitals are hurry up and wait most of the time, so that in and of itself is exhausting to me. The doctors shared more information on Dad's condition. They gave us every reason to believe Dad was going to fully recover, but Saturday was a hard day for him. He was highly agitated.

Dad told us that every time he closed his eyes, he could see the tire spinning over his head. He knew that if the truck went over his head, he would die. I had never seen my daddy deal with anxiety like this before. This was a first for me. Dad has a sanguine personality and is quite confident in the God he serves. I am not saying he had never experienced anxiety, but I never witnessed him dealing with this level of anxiety before that day. I wanted to soothe his spirit so badly. I wanted to help him find peace in the middle of the miracle. I just had no words. All I could do was smile big, hold his hand, and pray hard. So, that is what I did at every visit.

Once while we were waiting for a visit with Dad that day, Kenneth and I spoke a few moments of another accident that happened at Apostolic Lighthouse many years ago, back in January of 2010.

On this day, Kenneth met Dad at the church to help replace the light fixtures in the foyer. Dad was to hold the light fixture while Kenneth went down to get his drill from his tool bag on the floor. The light fixture was heavy which caused Dad to drop it. The sharp edge sliced Kenneth's right arm to the bone nearly severing an artery. With every heartbeat, blood spurted over the entire foyer like something out of a horror film. That day, Dad rushed Kenneth to the Emergency Room at Minden Medical Center. Out of all of us, Kenneth could most relate to Dad's post-traumatic stress.

Kenneth told me that for months every time he closed his eyes, he could see that fixture flying by his head.

To this day, Kenneth only has about 70% use of that hand and arm. His life was forever changed that moment the fixture fell. At the Emergency Room of Minden Medical Center, the doctor was unable to stop the artery from bleeding. Kenneth was eventually transferred to a hospital in Shreveport where a surgeon reattached the artery to the best of his ability and sewed up his arm.

We spent an exceedingly long, awful night at that hospital. The medicine they gave Kenneth after the surgery simply went into his skin rather than in his vein. The nurse either did not believe Kenneth or did not care. You could clearly see how swollen Kenneth's arm was. He felt no relief at all from the severe pain of having his arm deeply cut that day. He did not sleep at all that night and was hurting badly the next morning. I had to leave him to go get showered and bring him clean clothes. Everything was soaked in blood, including the floorboard of Dad's truck. His jeans, socks, and boots were all unsalvageable from the ugly black blood stains.

When I returned to the hospital, I was able to take Kenneth home. After months of therapy, he was able to return to work. The thought echoed through my head from the night before;

'What a difference a day makes.'

The light fixture changed Kenneth's life just as the truck changed Dad's life. Only Dad would not be going home today or any day soon. The doctors had already shared how amazed they were at the minimal damage Dad suffered. One of them stated that when they did the scans, she expected to find a multitude of more problems than the scans revealed. The eye doctor shared his skepticism on several occasions that Dad was doing so well after his orbital bone was crushed. This doctor even stayed in the ICU all night long that first night to do pressure checks on the injured eye every two hours. He could not understand how any of this was possible, but my family all knew that day that God had spared Dad for a purpose just as He had spared Kenneth nine years earlier.

Finally, we got word that Dad would be moved to a regular room. For me, this was a clear sign that he was making great progress! Sometime after lunch, Kenneth headed home to study and prepare for Sunday School. Kenneth and I were scheduled on this Saturday to be at one of the nursing homes in Minden; Town & Country Health & Rehab, to have church. However, I asked Kenneth to come be with me at the hospital instead.

While Dad was in ICU, I needed him to be with me. Once we knew Dad was moving to a regular room, Kenneth and I knew that Dad would be concerned about the services on Sunday. At that time, Kenneth was in the middle of teaching an anointed series of lessons called 'Ascend' about the Tabernacle of the Old Testament and why it matters to the church today. He was already on the calendar to teach Sunday School that morning. Additionally, Brother Charles Williams was already scheduled to preach Sunday night. God is never surprised or caught off guard. Perhaps we did not know that Dad would be in the hospital on Sunday, February 17, 2019, but God did.

I remember when Kenneth kissed me goodbye before he left that hospital that day, I felt a lurch in my stomach. I was dealing with a great deal of anxiety and suddenly I wondered if any of us would make it through this day. Immediately, I began to speak Scriptures to my mind. This was just not the time to fall apart. My family needs me.

Dad had several visitors that day. News of the accident

seemed to spontaneously combust across Louisiana and the entire organization of the Assemblies of the Lord Jesus Christ. Dad has been a part of this organization for almost all my life. He has always faithfully served God as an evangelist and pastor while simultaneously holding various positions within the organization to faithfully serve his brethren to the best of his abilities. A stream of visitors passed through the hospital that day while Mother, Karrah, James, Kenneth and I hurried up and waited.

As it began to get dark, Dad was himself enough that he started fussing about us being in that neighborhood at night. None of us brought up the fact that we had been there extremely late the night before. We all just silently agreed to let him be Dad and fuss. My second cousin, Lexi McDaniel and her husband Caleb, arrived earlier that afternoon to visit Dad. So, when he began to want us to go home so that we would not be there at night; we all decided to go have dinner together.

The atmosphere at that table that night was incredible for me. We were all simply grateful Dad was alive. Although the road to recovery was going to be long, he was going to recover. A peace fell on my soul as I sat there eating with my family.

What a difference a day makes. "I may not know what tomorrow holds, but I do know who holds tomorrow," I heard Dad say this millions of times throughout my life. Only now was I beginning to clearly understand what that meant. Your entire life can change in one second, one moment, one phone call, one blink of an eye.

What a difference a day makes!

Sunday

I was tired Sunday morning. I was disappointed that there would be no music at service. We tried to schedule a piano player, but she did not come. Church without music is hard. Music is essential to the worship service. Without it, the flesh must fight twice as hard to operate in the spirit. I was excited to see the church house full. I think almost the entire church family was gathered under one roof that morning. Kenneth was incredibly anointed that morning as he delivered the Word of God.

The presence of the Lord filled the place from the moment we began to pray that morning. We praised God for sparing Pastor's life while we sought His healing hands to soothe Pastor's pain. I will never forget the way I felt in church that morning. I held Kenneth's hand on our way to the hospital after church and was overwhelmed by one emotion after another. By the time we arrived at the hospital, I was more tired than when I woke up that morning. Dad looked like he was in so much pain that Sunday. He pulled Kenneth close and asked him very seriously; 'How was church, son?' My husband was incredibly happy to report to Dad how God showed up and filled the place with His presence. You could see Dad visibly relax on his hospital bed.

Karrah and James had to go home Sunday afternoon. They are only four hours away, but sometimes that four hours feels like a million miles. They had to go back to their life, but I knew how much I was going to miss my sister over the next few weeks and months. I hugged her tight wishing as always that she lived closer to me. I asked her to be sure and hug Madigan, Sara, Jaken, and Jymma tight for me. I love being an aunt, and I love my nieces and nephew ridiculously much. I treasure any time I have with them. As she left that day, I wondered exactly how I was supposed to get through all this without her.

By this time, Dad had shared his story with us of what had happened in the parking lot of Apostolic Lighthouse on that fateful Friday. That entire week had been incredibly busy. He taught Bible Study Wednesday night, then worked hard at the strawberry fundraiser all day Thursday. He was the last one to leave Thursday evening, and he was weary when he locked up the church. Everyone was tired.

When he awoke Friday morning, he spent time in prayer and sat down to rest up. He knew he would be able to prepare for the weekend services on Saturday, so he was feeling no rush to go anywhere or do anything which is a bit unusual. Dad told us, "Little did I know that morning that my life was about to change. I was not feeling very energetic. So, I told your mother I was just going to rest all day so I would be reenergized for the weekend services, but around 10:00 a.m. I received a phone call from Sudden Link letting me know the technician was at the church ready to install our new internet and phone system. I told the dispatcher I would be there in about fifteen minutes.

When I arrived, I met Mr. Sam Miller, the technician with Sudden Link. He informed me that the trailer we used to wash our strawberries the day before was in the way of where he needed to run cables into the church. I made two phone calls, but I was unsuccessful in reaching the man that owned the trailer. I hoped he would come get it or send someone to pick it up, but when I could not reach him, I decided to move the trailer myself because the church needed the phone and internet services.

I hooked my truck up to the trailer and begin to move it around to the other side of the church. All was going well until I pulled up a slight incline and put the truck in reverse to back the trailer up to the sidewalk. The trailer uncoupled from the hitch on the truck. I did not put on the chains because I was not going on the road with the trailer. I was only moving it in the parking lot from one side of the church to the other.

I put the truck in park and began to work my way to the trailer to grab the hitch and swing the trailer toward the church yard to keep it from going into the busy road in front of the church. Just as I turned the trailer enough to keep it from going into the street, my life changed. The truck jumped out of park into reverse and blindsided me in my chest, knocked me to the ground, and began to run over me.

I heard every bone from the base of my head to my hips popping. Pain gripped my body as the right rear passenger tire began to go up the left side of my face. I realized I was in trouble, so I began to holler for help.

In just a moment, two men arrived. One held my head in a towel and the other told me to lay still. He told me I would be all right. He repeated that several times in a soothing voice. Finally, Sam with Sudden Link came running from the other side of the building. The man who was telling me to lay still told Sam to get in the truck and that he would guide him so he could drive the truck off me and not hurt me anymore. As Sam moved the truck, first responders arrived. As the first responders began to work with me, those two men that had arrived first disappeared as quietly and quickly as they appeared.

Blood was pouring out of my nose, eyes, ears, and mouth. I could hear the concern in the voices of the men and women who were trying to help me. When they turned me to my back, my left eye fell into my nasal cavity. They begin to try and find veins into which they could start an IV so they would be able to give me medicine to relief the pain, but they were unable to do so. They decided to try something else.

They were drilling a hole in my shin when I began fighting them. I heard someone say, 'Restrain him!' When they did, they gave me medicine that knocked me out for the life flight ride in the helicopter.

I don't remember leaving Minden Medical Center, but I do remember landing at Oschner LSU Health Shreveport. People were rushing around me and I was nauseated and in what felt like unendurable pain. I began to have trouble breathing and started to vomit.

When your mother finally came into the room yesterday, peace came over me. I thought maybe I will make it, because I was not sure a few times."

When my brother-in-law checked the truck, there was one small dent in the truck's right rear bumper where it struck the trailer. We believe the trailer along with the hand of God stopped the truck from completely running over Dad's head. The doctor told us it was a good thing Dad has such a hard head and thick chest because if he were a smaller man, the truck would have run all the way over him and there was no way he would have survived. However, I believe that the fervent prayers of the saints birthed the miracle of dads survival. No matter what happened in the parking lot of Apostolic Lighthouse that morning, God saved him that afternoon.

Since the accident, we asked every police officer and first responder on the scene if they got the names of the first two men who helped Dad while the truck was still on him.

All the officials know who we are talking about, remember seeing them, and they can even describe those men, but no one knows their names. Several officers stated they wrote the names in their reports. Therefore, we reviewed the reports, but there is no mention of these men and their names are not there. Until we find them, we can only believe they were angels sent to minister to Dad until help arrived.

I wanted to be with Dad Sunday night, but he wanted me to go to church. Kenneth also wanted me to be with him at church. The Williams preached that night, and most of the church people came again. We were all rejoicing in the miracle that Dad was alive after being pinned underneath a moving vehicle on Friday.

I remember Sister Donna Jo Hall (Gavin Hall's mother) testified of the amazing miracle that Dad was alive. She works in the medical field as a CRNA (Certified Registered Nurse Anesthetist). This field of work uniquely qualifies her to understand when a medical miracle happens. One of the things I learned from her testimony is that it takes much more pressure to break a human bone than to burst a blood vessel. Dad's left orbital bone and nose were broken, yet he (a heart patient on blood thinners) had no brain bleed!!! According to Sister Hall, this is a miracle!

Rejoicing broke out among all of us in the building as we thanked God for sparing our Pastor.

After church, I had to go home. I had to return to work Monday morning and sleep is vital to my ability to function at work. That night sleep came swiftly and deep as I prayed for Dad to recover from this trauma that would forever change his life. The realization that life would never be quite the same again kept flowing through my mind. Dad will always divide his life between "before the truck" and "after the truck." I cannot remember the dreams I had, but I dreamed all night because I went back to work the next day feeling like I had a hangover.

Hospital Life

When I went back to work, I requested to be off for Dad's surgery which was scheduled for Friday, February 22, 2019. Everyone at Evergreen was incredibly kind and supportive during that whole week. I was in a crazy routine. I would get to the office as early as possible; I would work my eight hours and get off and rush to the hospital. Except I usually did not go straight to the hospital. I always tried to bring Dad something from outside that depressing place. I brought anything he may be need or want to make his day a little brighter. One day I may stop at the drug store, the next day I may stop at Griff's for a chocolate milkshake. I did anything I could to lift the spirits of this battered and bruised man in that hospital bed.

I ate several evenings at the hospital dining room. I was beginning to feel as though I lived at the hospital. At night I went home showered and dropped in bed feeling as though every bit of strength and energy were zapped by the day. During this period, I remember several of Dad's visitors from Apostolic Lighthouse reminded him of times past when God protected his life at the church. You see, Dad is a worker. Unfortunately, he can be an impatient worker. Sometimes, rather than waiting for help, he will tackle jobs on his own. At times this is an admirable trait, but there are times this is dangerous.

For example, in May 2012, work was being done in the kitchen and fellowship hall of Apostolic Lighthouse. There is not much space to serve meals, so the church decided to remodel a bit to make better use of the small space. A crew was supposed to meet Dad at the church at 7:00 a.m. to begin work one morning. At 8:00 a.m., the crew was not there. Dad looked around and found a job that he felt he could do on his own to help move along the remodel. There was a receptacle that needed to be moved up to plug in food warmers for serving. Dad plugged a fan into this receptacle, but the fan had no power. Then, he plugged in a drill with the same result. This led Dad to believe that the power had been cut to the receptacle by the crew and it would be safe to remove the receptacle on his own.

At this point, Dad noticed the box was metal rather than plastic. Because the power was cut, the material of the box was irrelevant. When Dad put his pliers in the metal box, electricity surged through his hands. The awful realization hit him full force that the receptacle was live! He was being electrocuted, and he was alone in the building with no help. Dad began to struggle against the powerful grip of raw electricity to let go of the pliers conducting that same electricity through his hands and arms to his body. Somehow, he was able to get his feet up on the wall and push himself off the receptacle. When he did, the force of the voltage threw Dad against the opposite wall of the fellowship hall.

His hands were burned and there were burns across his chest, but his heart was beating. The church family of Apostolic Lighthouse became adamant that Pastor was never allowed to work alone at the church again! In the future, he must be patient and wait for help to arrive. Everyone felt a sense of relief that this brush with danger was fleeting and without any long-term consequences. However, in September of 2016, Dad once again was working at the church alone. This time, he was in the attic above the women's restroom at the front of Apostolic Lighthouse. There was a strong sewer smell every time it rained because the restroom was not vented correctly. Dad knew how to fix it and decided on this day to get the job done! Mother told me once that she decided Dad is helping the Lord keep her on her knees in prayer!

He did not follow the mandate of the people of Apostolic Lighthouse to wait for help because all the members of the church are hard working men and women with busy schedules. Dad was not sure how long he would have to wait for someone to be available to come help. Since he knew how to do the job, why wait? I will share with you why I wish he would have waited for help. When Dad stepped from one beam to the next, he missed the step and fell through the ceiling of the women's restroom. Dad was able to grab the rafter as he fell and hold himself until he got his feet planted onto the stall wall below him. Then he sat on top of the stall wall and turned where he could slide down the wall to floor. The grace of God allowed my Dad to have the strength to grab that rafter, keep himself from falling, and hold himself there until he could stabilize on the stall wall below rather than crashing straight to the floor below possibly breaking every bone in his body.

If you are keeping track, the truck is the fourth physical attack on ministry at Apostolic Lighthouse. In 2010, Dad dropped the light fixture on Kenneth and Kenneth could have bled to death in the foyer of the church. In 2012, Dad was electrocuted and if he had not pushed himself off the receptacle in the fellowship hall, he could have died alone that day in the fellowship hall of the church. In 2016, Dad fell through the ceiling of the women's restroom and could have easily fallen all the way to the ceramic tile floor resulting in serious injuries. In 2019, a truck ran over my Dad in the parking lot and could have killed him. I believe the enemy does not want Apostolic Lighthouse to exist. He has actively attacked the ministry to destroy the church. There must be a reason God has spared the lives of my husband and my dad. I cannot begin to fathom why He allowed these attacks on my loved ones, but I can tell you that each time God stepped on the scene and kept them. I stand in awe of his grace and mercy every time I look at the faces of these men I love.

"...When the enemy shall come in like a flood, the Spirit of the Lord shall lift up a standard against him."

(Isaiah 59:19)

Marsha

The day before the surgery, Mother called me before I got to the hospital. She told me that she wanted me to meet a woman named Marsha. The social anxiety disorder means I need notice when meeting new people. I need time to adjust to the idea so that the meeting will go well. I need information. Mother told me that she met a Pentecostal woman named Hope Guerrero in the elevator. Hope told Mother about her sister, Marsha. The meeting between Hope and Mother that day was no accident or coincidence. There is a purpose in pain and these two ladies had to meet to reveal the purpose of the pain two souls were enduring on the trauma floor of the hospital that cold day.

Marsha was in the hospital in a room on the same floor right around the corner from Dad's room. Marsha was suffering from uterine cancer that had spread throughout her body. Hope later shared with me that Marsha initially went to the doctor with severe back pain. The first doctor diagnosed her with bulging discs and gave her injections which worked for a few days, but the pain quickly returned intensified. When Marsha returned to the doctor, he told her that she could not have any more injections for a while and there was nothing to worry about because his diagnosis was firm. All that was wrong with her was bulging discs.

Marsha decided to get a second opinion because she knew something was not right. The second doctor did a pelvic exam and found the uterine cancer. When he examined her back, this doctor told Marsha she had a visible tumor. She was an extremely sick woman. By the time I met Marsha on February 20, 2019, she had undergone a complete hysterectomy and colostomy. She was in constant, severe pain.

Though we serve a loving God, He cares more about our character than our comfort. God cares more about our souls than the physical house in which they live. God had a purpose for Marsha's pain. The prognosis was grim. The cancer had rapidly spread throughout her entire body. Hope told us that Marsha was not just her sister, she was also her best friend. Sister Guerrero said they had contacted a local church because Marsha had decided she needed to pray, and she wanted someone to pray with her and for her. The person who answered the phone at the church told Hope they would send someone from their ministry team to the hospital to pray with Marsha. The sisters waited, but no one ever came.

When Hope and Mother met in the elevator, Mother immediately agreed to go pray for Marsha. Mother said when she prayed for Marsha, she felt God working on her soul, but there was no breakthrough. That is when she asked if I could come and pray for Marsha the next time I was at the hospital. The sisters happily agreed. Hope told us on several occasions she feels like Mother was an answer to prayer that day. God was working to reveal His purpose in the midst of Marsha's pain.

I had to stop and pray as soon as my mother, who is also my pastor's wife, called me and told me that she wanted me to meet and pray for Marsha. This kind of interaction is way out of my comfort zone. Sometimes in a powerful church service when the Holy Ghost is moving, I feel God whisper to me to pray for someone I know. In that situation, I can confidently pray for them knowing God is attentive. After all, I am only doing what He asked me to do. However, praying for a stranger in an impersonal hospital room was a bit daunting to me. I asked God to lead and guide me as I told Mother I would be happy to pray for Marsha. When I got to the hospital, I barely got to speak to Dad before Mother insisted that we go meet Marsha.

When we walked in that hospital room, the first thing I thought was that I was happy there was no roommate in there. I was thankful when we prayed there would be no faithless spectators. Mother introduced me to Hope Guerrero and Marsha Brumley, then she ran back to Dad's room leaving me on my own.

I took a deep breath and began to talk with these two sweet sisters who were fighting physical and spiritual battles of great magnitude. Most of that conversation is a big blur now. At one point, Marsha told me that she could not go back to God because she had gone too far, too long. I shared some of my testimony with her because I am a recovered backslider. I know exactly how it feels to go too far from God for too long. I also know that there is no such thing as too far, too long. I know this is a lie from the pits of hell specifically designed to keep souls from returning to God.

After talking a while, I asked Marsha to pray with me. Hope, Marsha, and I joined hands and began to pray. At first, mostly Hope and I were praying for Marsha and interceding on her behalf as she struggled to find words to express herself to God. In a few moments, Marsha joined us. I heard her telling God how much she loved Him. I heard her say she missed God. All backsliders miss God. We never talk about it, but backsliders long for restoration and peace. Of course, when humanity seeks the Lord, He always shows up! Soon, the Holy Ghost filled her hospital room on the trauma floor of Oschner LSU Health Shreveport.

I remember she put her hand over her mouth one time while we were praying. So, I told her that God would never force Himself upon her, but He was here. If she wanted the Holy Ghost, all she had to do was open her mouth and speak in tongues. We began to pray again and that is exactly what she did! Marsha raised her hands right there in the middle of all her pain and opened her mouth and spoke in a beautiful heavenly language of worship and praise to Almighty God!

I am not sure how long we rejoiced and basked in the presence of God that afternoon. When we finished praying, I hugged my new friends. Marsha told me that she was ready now. Whether or not God healed her was suddenly secondary to the assurance that she had found the purpose to her pain. She was saved! Heaven was sure!

I rushed back to Dad's room. I was weeping as I burst through his door. "She prayed through! I prayed her through! She got the Holy Ghost!" Everything came rushing out at once. Mother and Dad both broke down and rejoiced with me that Marsha's name was once again in the Lamb's Book of Life. All of Heaven rejoiced with us that a sinner had repented and returned to God. The three of us agreed in that room that afternoon that this was the purpose for Dad's pain. We were sent to that place at that time to help Marsha make things right with God.

The next time Kenneth was at the hospital, we went over and prayed with Marsha again. They were still rejoicing in the Holy Ghost. Hope told us that Marsha was a changed woman. They were praying and singing together continually.

We kept in contact with these precious sisters after Dad was released from Oschner LSU Health Shreveport back to Minden Medical Center Rehab. Hope told me when Marsha was released from the hospital, she went home on hospice. Every day she listened to Christian music and spent time in prayer. At night, Hope could hear her sister speaking in tongues as she tried in vain to find sleep or a few moments of relief from the unrelenting pain. The night before Marsha died, Hope told her, "Go home, Marsha. God wants you. He loves you. You are ready. Go home."

That same night, Marsha kept talking to area at the foot of her bed. "Are y'all here to get me? I'm ready to go. You can take me now." When her loved ones questioned her, Marsha told them she was talking to the angels down there. The angels were there to take her home.

The next morning, Marsha took her medicine and went to sleep for the last time. She will spend eternity worshiping around the throne of God. The purpose of her pain was the salvation of her soul. Yes, I believe God values your soul more than your body. He will do whatever it takes to save your soul. There is nothing more important to God than salvation of your soul.

Surgery

Friday finally arrived. I got to the hospital early and Mother was already there! She is not an early riser, but she said she got there around 6:00 a.m. that morning. We waited for the surgery team to come get Dad. They showed up around 8:00 a.m. and we prayed together for Dad before they rolled him away to put a titanium plate in his face to hold up his eye. Up until now, Dad had severe double vision which caused dizziness and nausea.

A few more hours went by before we got word, that they finally started the surgery around 11:20 a.m. Mother and I discussed how we hope Dad will remember who was there on surgery day. We want to help him remember those who sacrificed to be with him. Love last forever.

The surgery only lasted about an hour. Doctors talked to Mother, and they are again surprised by how well Dad did. Because Dad was going to be in recovery a while, Mother decided to go home and get a few things to spend the night. She usually does not spend the night with Dad, but she decided to do so that night. I stayed to wait for Dad to get out of recovery and be with him until Mother returned. She was not gone long when they rolled Dad into his room. He was soon conscious, and he was hurting badly.

I asked for pain meds for him, and the nurse said she would get something for him. We began the waiting game. A while later, I reminded the nurse he was waiting for meds because he was loudly moaning and groaning in pain. Additionally, he had not had anything to eat or drink since midnight and I knew he was hungry, thirsty, and in agonizing pain. After the second request, Dad started talking out of his head. He was talking about someone beating him in the head. I assured him no one was beating him.

Dad's room was across the hall from the nursing station. I went and stood at the door of his room watching the staff hang out at the nursing station not doing much of anything that I could tell. I did not see the nurse anywhere. After a few moments, an aide attempted to come in the room to take Dad's blood pressure, but I had to get Dad the medicine he needed. I told her they would not be doing anything else until Dad got some pain meds. I told the aide Dad was talking out of his head and his nurse had disappeared. The aide stated that the nurse was helping another patient and not able to bring Dad anything right now. I told her that was no excuse as I had already notified the nurse twice of Dad's need. I was not rude, but I was unmovable. There would be no blood pressure taken until Dad received his pain meds.

In just a few minutes, the nurse showed up out of nowhere with Dad's medicine. I thanked her, but I could tell she was aggravated. The young nurse told me that she was working in another room and unable to bring the medicine until just now. Attempting to remain polite, I reminded her that this was the third request for his medication. If she had brought the medicine when he first needed it, perhaps this incident could have been avoided. I genuinely appreciated her help and all her hard work during this tension filled time. I went back to Dad's bedside and assured him everything was fine. I was just making sure his medications were in order.

The nurse refused to give Dad a shot for his pain and rather gave him medicine orally, so it took a good while to kick in. During that time, Dad fervently talked about his passion to be one of the good men for God. Over and over, he told me he wanted to be one of the good men of God. He told me that Bishop Steve Wilson had visited him. Bishop Wilson had visited a few days before on Wednesday, but in his surgery addled mind the visit seemed like it just happened. He also told me of other visitors that had come throughout the week.

Dad seemed to be getting some encouragement from reliving the visits from people who love him. He was distracting his body from the pain somewhat while we waited for the medicine to kick in. I hoped the medication would give him some relief and rest. I held Dad's hand and prayed for him to have peace and healing. Soon he was still. His eyes were closed. He was not asleep, but he was peaceful. About an hour later, he finally was asleep, and I laid down on the small visitor's bed beside him. I was exhausted from advocating for my Dad's health in a tough environment.

Mother arrived and I shared with her the incident and what it took to get Dad the medication he needed. This caused her to be even more worried than she already was about what kind of care Dad would receive the night of his surgery. We prayed together that they would have a good night and Dad would rest well. Kenneth came to the hospital when he got off from work to check on Dad, and prayed with us again. I was worn out, so I decided to go eat in the cafeteria and head home. As I left the hospital alone that night, I felt a loneliness steal into my soul. I knew on a logical plane that I was surrounded by support, but in that moment alone in my vehicle the night of the surgery, my soul ached. I was also a bit concerned about how the night of surgery would be for my parents. Hospitals can be tough places to be especially if the staff is not kind or compassionate.

That night, Dad had an amazing nurse named Starla. Up to this point, there had been a few negative interactions with the nursing staff. For example, the first night that Dad was in the ICU, the nurse refused to suction him after he coughed up excessive phlegm. She insisted he do it himself with one broken shoulder and one fractured shoulder. This woman seemed to be ill and working anyway, but clearly quite angry about it. She took out her personal frustration on my Dad when he needed her compassion and care at one of the lowest points in his life.

Then, during the night a few times that week, Dad would call for help with no response. These incidents are why Mother decided to stay with Dad the night of the surgery against his vehement wishes that she be home by dark every evening.

After the issue with Dad's medication, I felt like we had made the right choice for Mother to stay. The sad reality was we were not sure what kind of care he may receive. That night God blessed Dad with a nurse who was the absolute epitome of professionalism, compassion, and kindness. She was a highly competent health care professional dedicated to impeccable patient care. Starla made an impact on my Dad's life that night. Mother and Dad told me later that it felt like she was an angel sent from Heaven. All through that night, every time he called for help, Starla was there immediately with a gentle touch and kind voice of concern.

The marked difference between the callous care of the ICU nurse and the compassionate care of Starla were the basis of Dad's first message about his survival preached in June of 2019 at First Apostolic Church in Maryland, Tennessee pastored by Rev. Kenneth Carpenter.

Earlier in the year, Mother spoke on Mother's Day at Apostolic Lighthouse a short thought titled; 'Calloused Saints or Compassionate Christians.' She shared some of the differences between the angry nameless nurse in the ICU and compassionate Starla. Mother encouraged the mothers of Apostolic Lighthouse to be compassionate Christians and guard themselves from becoming calloused saints. Dad built on the remarks Mother gave and shared his testimony for the first time under the title 'Compassionate Christian.' This message can be found on the Facebook page of First Apostolic Church of Maryville, Tennessee. Dad was anointed by the Lord as he delivered the Word of God in that service.

His story can never truly be told by anyone else. When Dad approached me to write down his story, I knew I could only tell you my part of it. If you want to hear the most powerful message of the miracle of Rev. Bill R. Mills, I encourage you to look up his message on Facebook today! You will be blessed beyond measure by his words.

My family will be eternally grateful for the nurse named Starla given to my dad by God the night of his surgery to reflect His compassion toward mankind. None of us want to become a calloused saint. The cares of life can weigh us down until we no longer feel compassion toward the lost souls of this world. Yet the last thing our world needs is one more calloused saint. The church must keep its compassion at all cost!

As the day of surgery ended, all of us drew a deep, collective breath of relief that Dad was recovering as well as could be expected given the trauma he endured just one short week ago. Once again, I went to sleep feeling grateful that

I still had my dad with me. The surgery was a success and the prognosis for full recovery was good. The man was a miracle. Both the eye doctor and the ICU doctor admitted my Dad is a true miracle.

Conclusion

Dad spent ten days at Minden Medical Center Rehab. I stopped making daily visits somewhere towards the end of his stay here. He was finally released from Minden Medical Center Rehab under home health on March 7, 2019 twenty days after the "the truck incident" changed his life. He was abundantly blessed with compassionate nurses and doctors throughout the rest of his recovery. Once he was discharged from Oschner LSU Health Shreveport, Dad never had another negative interaction with any healthcare workers.

He worked hard at rehab and gave 100% during every single

therapy session he endured to regain mobility of his arms and shoulders.

Dad was longing to get back to the house of God. One Monday morning, he told Mother I am going to church Sunday. He worked hard all week, and on March 31, 2019 Dad was able to come to Apostolic Lighthouse and worship with the saints of God. He briefly addressed the congregation and reminded us that Jesus Christ holds the power of life and death in His hands. Dad told us he was only standing before us because of the string of miracles God wove together for His glory.

For many years, Dad prayed for a miracle to let all of Minden know that Apostolic Lighthouse is the place to run when you need a miracle. He had no idea God would make him the miracle. He did not know the purpose of his pain was to see a woman named Marsha filled with the Holy Ghost. He did know it was worth it all. He told us that he planned to preach his first message on Easter.

When April 21, 2019 rolled around and Apostolic Lighthouse gathered to celebrate Resurrection Sunday, Dad preached his first message since the accident. He stood under the anointing of the Holy Ghost and preached a message titled "Hope in a Promise."

All of Apostolic Lighthouse rejoiced over the power that raised Jesus from the grave and saved Dad from the grave that morning!

Back in January 2006, I helped my Dad write an article for the Apostolic Witness titled 'Daily Miracles.' To conclude this narrative, I would like to share an excerpt from that article with you. "Every day miracles occur all around us. Only the spiritually sensitive or truly observant among us recognize these seemingly everyday happenings as miracles. What is a miracle? The dictionary defines a miracle as "an event or action that apparently contradicts known scientific laws" or "a remarkable thing." My definition of miracle is "an act of God." Man cannot perform miracles. The source of every miracle is Jesus Christ. Each and every act of God is a miracle. Large or small, every time God acts, the result is a miracle!

In my ministry, I have been blessed to witness many miracles. I have seen people healed. I have seen people filled. I have seen people delivered and set free! If anyone is around the true church for very long, they will encounter the supernatural, extraordinary acts of God that one and all recognize as miraculous.

…The God I serve is omnipotent. He will not share His power with another. The power of God is without limitation. The human mind is incapable of fully grasping the depth of that kind of power.

There are some today that do not believe miracles still happen. That mankind can be this deceived is incomprehensible to me. The desperation that undoubtedly accompanies this deception results in life without love, hope, or peace. In reality, the result is no life at all. Life without God is just not life. Life itself is a gift from God; therefore, an act of God. If life is an act of God, life is a miracle.

How do you define a miracle? If your definition of a miracle is limited to events or actions that apparently contradict known scientific laws, then you are missing the miracles all around you. The sunrise every morning is a miracle. No man can make the sun rise or set; therefore, it is an act of God. The rainbow after the storm is a miracle. Only God can place the rainbow in the sky; therefore, the rainbow is a miracle. Every day of your life there is a miracle waiting to be discovered. Determine in your heart to find the miracle God has for you today. The miracle may be one of the supernatural, extraordinary sort or just the simple act of God in your life for today. Just remember that each and every time God acts, the result is a miracle!"

"Have you had your miracle today?"

Marsha is not the only soul that will be in Heaven as a result of the traumatic accident my Dad experienced. There is a revival of souls coming through the doors of Apostolic Lighthouse. Many of them will come just because they heard the pastor got ran over by a truck and lived to preach about it. Many of them will come searching for a miracle. Some may come because they read this account want their pain to have a purpose. Some may come because they finally fully understand what a difference a day makes. I hope someone will come because they read about Marsha and finally stopped believing the lie that they are too far, too long gone. Most of all, I pray you now know beyond a shadow of a doubt miracles are real.

See For Yourself

The truck's only damage:

One Small Dent.

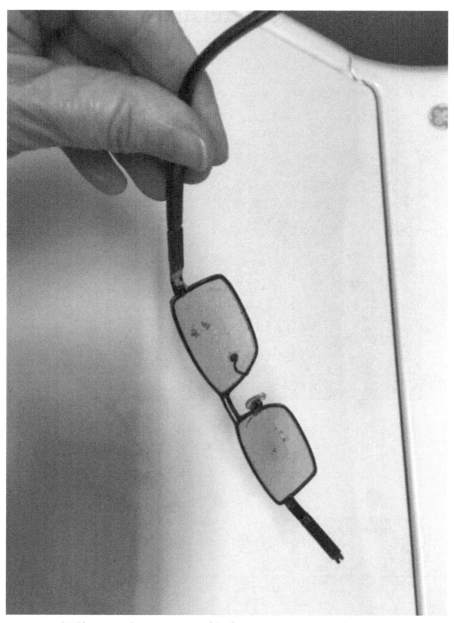

The glasses did not survive...

The Aftermath

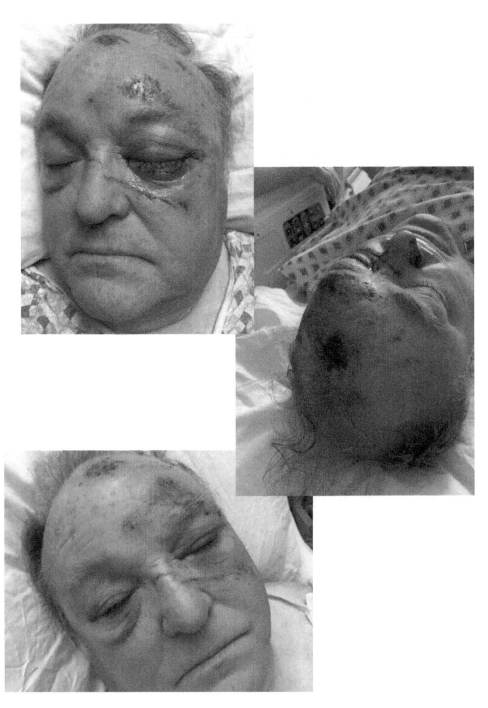

Dad opened his left eye for the first time!

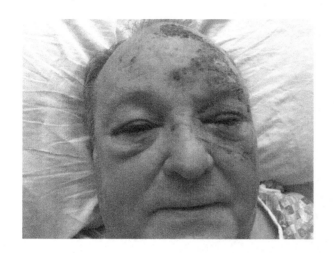

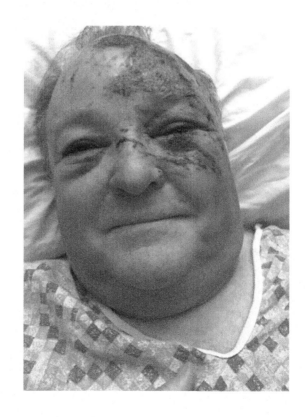

Dr. Byrd and Dr. Shaukat
both declared my dad to be a miracle!

Minden pastor thankful after accident

JULIUNA ANDERSON
janderson@press-herald.com

The Rev. Bill Mills, pastor of Apostolic Lighthouse Church was involved in a serious accident February 16 outside of the church involving a truck and a trailer. He is currently in the hospital recuperating.

Mills did not want to go into the details of the accident but wanted thank Sam Miller of Suddenlink for his quick response in helping Mills and the first responders who Mills says saved his life.

"I want him to know how much I'm thankful for what he did," Mills said.

"I want to personally thank the first responders and the emergency room at Minden, I didn't know if I would have made it without their quick response. They ought to get some kind of award from the city," said Mills.

Mills said he hopes to meet with the first responders at Grace Estates when he has recovered to thank them for their assistance.

"If the first responders had not been as diligent and as quick as they were there's a good possibility that I would not have been here," Mills said.

Mills was a candidate in the most recent City Council race for District E. He has been the pastor of Apostolic Lighthouse Church for 11 years.

Lakeside s Washington

From left, Scotts Electric's Emma involved in the p

Lakeside

Special to the Minde

Lakeside's Junior, done it again. For the nd consecutive year and fourth time in six years, side will be sending st dens to Washington

The Amazing
Minden Medical Rehab Team
who worked tirelessly to ensure Dad's recovery!

Interview - Anonymus

In preparation for writing this book, I interviewed some key witnesses to my Dad's miracle. The first interview I did was by phone with a friend of my parents. Mother met a hospice chaplain in 2010 when my precious grandmother was placed in hospice care. On 02/20/2020 around 6:11 p.m., I called this woman who prayed diligently for my Dad before anyone even knew he was in an accident.

The first thing I asked her was "Since the accident was on 02/15/2019 (just over a year ago), how clearly do you remember this incident?" The reply came back quickly that she remembered very clearly that day and that she did not think she could ever forget it. Next, I simply asked her to relay the events of that day in her own words however she wanted to share them.

"It was a Friday morning, and I was studying my Bible as usual. Somewhere between 9:00 a.m. and 10:00 a.m., I heard sirens. We live near the local hospital so this not unusual. Anytime I hear the sirens, I pray for whatever may be happening. On this day, the intensity of the sirens was unusual, so I prayed harder.

In Numbers 10:9, God tells his people; "And if ye go to war in your land against the enemy that opresseth you, then ye shall blow an alarm with the trumpets; and ye shall be remembered before the LORD your God, and ye shall be saved from your enemies." As I entered intercession, I began to walk around our small home and blow upon my shofar. We call our home the Prayer Cottage because we fill it with prayer continually.

Next, I felt the Lord tell me to bind the Spirit of Death. This has only happened a few times in my life. I was home alone and the intense burden to bind the Spirit of Death was upon me. I was fighting deep and intense spiritual warfare. This is when I heard the helicopter. I did not know who I was praying for, but I knew it was serious.

In a little while, Dana called me to cancel an appointment and asked me to pray for Brother Bill because he had been in an accident and was airlifted to Shreveport. I told her I had already been praying. Now I finally knew what I was praying about, so I continued in a spirit of prayer for a long while. I love these folks, and I was incredibly thankful to intercede for Brother Bill. I am happy for his recovery. I am grateful I was able to stand in the gap during his time of his need."

The last question I asked was "Do you believe Bill Mills is a miracle?" The answer was a resounding YES! I asked this question at the end of all of the interviews I was blessed to conduct while writing down Dad's miracle and as you will see, every time the answer is unequivocally yes.

Interview - Gavin Hall

I met with Gavin after Sunday School in the fellowship hall of Apostolic Lighthouse on September 20, 2020 around 11:30 a.m. I asked Mother to join us and record his interview in case my notes missed anything. Mother was happy to join us.

I began the interview with Gavin the same as the first interview; "Because so much time has passed since the accident, how well do you remember that day, 02/15/2019?" Gavin was quick to respond that he remembered the day perfectly. I asked him to share his thoughts and memories of that day however he wanted.

Gavin was packed up to go to a ball tournament in South Louisiana that weekend. He was at the barber shop getting a haircut when he got a call that there was a bad accident in Minden. As soon as he got out of the barber's chair, he headed to Minden Medical Center to help with the trauma. This is a small hospital completely unequipped to handle catastrophic medical emergencies. The room had easily fifteen to eighteen people working on the patient on the table. Gavin was given his task to perform for the team. At the time, he had no idea who the patient was lying there on the gurney. He told me that all he remembered thinking was how odd that this man was screaming in pain, but not cursing or using any foul language as he usually heard from people. His phone rang, but he declined the call from his mother and returned to the work of trying to save a life.

The phone immediately rang again, and it was his mother again. This time he gruffly answered the phone with a bit of an attitude because he was working. "What is it, Mom?" Sister Hall was extremely concerned and told Gavin he must get to the church as soon as possible because Pastor Mills had been hit by a vehicle. Gavin hung up and checked the bay of Minden Medical Center and realized that all the ambulances were there. He walked back to the room of the trauma and asked the name of the patient. That was the moment he realized the man he had been trying to help was his pastor. He said that Dad was sedated to insert a breathing tube. Gavin walked with the gurney outside and met the flight crew. At this point, he asked for the trauma team to pray with him for his pastor. "We all know there is only so much we can do, let's turn to the One who can do anything."

He returned to Minden Medical Center and made phone calls to inform the church family and those close to him about what was happening to Dad. He called my mother and told her not to come to Minden Medical Center because Dad was being taken by life flight to Oschner LSU Health Shreveport. He said that she was not happy with Dad because he was moving that trailer by himself. If he would have just waited for help, this would have never happened! Gavin felt like she had no idea how serious the accident was. He also made another call to his mother, but Sister Hall was unable to communicate in English as she was interceding for her pastor by praying in other tongues in the Holy Ghost. He told the church members that called him that they should go to the hospital if they could.

When he got to the Emergency Room at Oschner LSU Health Shreveport, he found Mother and me in the tiny family waiting room for trauma patients. Gavin said that

Mother and I left the room together at one point and he leaned over to the other ladies in the room and asked them to pray. He said, "They don't really understand how bad this is." Gavin told us that a little while later I came rushing in the room talking about a foot. "She swore she saw her Daddy's foot." I laughed and told him that I did see my Daddy's foot! Soon, they allowed us to see Pastor Mills for a moment. Gavin distinctly remembered the change that swept over my mother when she saw my dad on that hospital bed. All her frustration melted instantly and was replaced with compassion and concern. When Dad was conscious and responding, Gavin felt a sense of relief wash over him.

Until then, after seeing the blood coming from his pastor's nose, ears, eyes, and mouth, he was not sure if the man could survive the trauma of having a truck crush the side of his head. This was the turning point for Gavin. Hope sprang up and he knew that prayer had already changed things. I ended my time with Gavin with the same question I asked in the first interview, "Do you think Dad is a miracle?" Gavin smiled and told me he knew Dad was a miracle. Because Dad was a heart patient on blood thinners, for him to have no brain bleeds after that type of serious head trauma was nothing short of a miracle. Truly his pastor is a walking, talking miracle!

Interview - Leah Rogers

I conducted a phone interview with Leah Rogers on January 20, 2021. Ms. Rogers was the lead paramedic on the ambulance that arrived at Apostolic Lighthouse on February 15, 2019 in response to the 911 call made by someone in the parking lot that day. Because so much time had passed between the date of the accident and the date of the interview with Ms. Rogers, I began by asking her if she clearly remembered the events of that day. Her response was that she remembered that call vividly. Leah stated that when everything turns into chaos around her, she gets calm and gets to work.

Ms. Rogers told me that when the call came in, they were not sure what to expect or what happened. They were told it was a MVA (Moving Vehicle Accident) with a pedestrian involved. Leah said they just did not know exactly what happened. When they got there, police were already on the scene along with a few witnesses. Leah mentioned the two men everyone saw, but she did not know their names or how to reach them. (She did think those two men are from Minden, so hopefully they will come forward if they read about themselves!) The truck was already moved off Dad when the ambulance arrived, so Leah started her assessment.

Dad was breathing and talking. He told her his name. They were able to get Dad on a gurney and get him into the ambulance. Leah immediately called for air transport, but it was thirty minutes out. She knew they had to keep Dad still. There was severe damage to his left side, and she was not sure what kind of internal damage he had. Leah was most concerned about his lungs because one or both could easily be deflated due to the trauma he had endured. However, Dad was hollering in pain; therefore, this was a good sign that he was breathing and getting oxygen.

Leah decided to get Dad to Minden Medical Center Emergency Room while they waited for air support because they needed more people and Dad needed an IV. They had to hold Dad's ankles down and drill a hole in his shin because they were unable to start the IV. When they did so, they gave him enough medicine to knock him out for the trip to Oschner LSU Health Shreveport. At this point, they intubated Dad and the flight crew arrived. They did their assessment and took Dad to the waiting helicopter.

I ended my interview with Ms. Rogers as I did the others. I asked her if she thought my Dad was a miracle. She said, "Yes!" Those kinds of calls do not always end well. Leah Rogers played a critical role in giving Dad the care he needed in the most important moments immediately following his accident. I am incredibly thankful that God put her there in that moment to minister to Dad. First responders are incredible people, and I am grateful I had a chance to speak with Ms. Rogers and thank her personally for the care she gave Dad.

Sam Miller

My goal was to finish this account with an interview with Mr. Sam Miller, the contractor from Sudden Link, who drove the truck off Dad. However, we lost touch with Mr. Miller somewhere along the way and have been unable to reach him to conduct the desired interview.

Therefore, I decided to write a short acknowledgement and simple thank you to this man. After the angels ministered to Dad, he was the next person on the scene to help save Dad's life.

Mr. Miller listened to exactly what the unknown man told him to do and drove the truck off Dad without causing any further injuries. I appreciate and respect Sam Miller more than simple words can convey. I pray *Miracle of Minden* will find its way into his hands one day and he will know that his actions that day forever made a difference in our lives. Thank you, sir. May God richly bless you and keep you all the days of your life is my sincere prayer.

Acknowledgements

Many people made this publication possible, and I want to thank all of them. I must start with my husband, Kenneth Greer. Thank you for supporting me during the writing of this project. I know I was not easy to live with, but you were always supportive that I could do this, and that *Miracle of Minden* is going to bless someone.

Next, I must thank my parents. Dad, thank you for trusting me with your story. I hope and pray I wrote it well, because this is an incredible testimony, and you deserve the best. Mother, you asked me to write a book many times. You believe in me when I do not. Thank you for your love and support.

Karrah, I cannot explain what you mean to me. You are the strongest woman I have ever known, and I am incredibly thankful you are a part of my life. More importantly, I genuinely appreciate you allowing me to be a part of your life. I love you, James, Madigan, Sara, Jaken, and Jymma deeply. You are not just my sister; you are my best friend.

I would also like to thank the people who took time to interview with me. Anonymous, you know who you are, and I appreciate your time. I believe your contribution made this project better. May God richly bless you is my prayer. Gavin, thank you for all you are to Apostolic Lighthouse and my dad. Thank you for your time and insight. We love and appreciate you very much. Leah, thank you very much for your perspective that day. I cannot thank you enough for the care you gave Dad when he needed it the most. Thank you with all my heart.

I must also thank Sister Donna Jo Hall for proofing my project. She made this work much better and saved me from looking goofy on several occasions! Thank you, my friend. Only God can reward you for all you do for His Kingdom. All of us are blessed to know you and because you are a part of our lives.

Finally, I must thank Brother David A. Moore for all his contributions to *Miracle of Minden*. The website and marketing that were donated to this project are priceless. Without your help, this project simply would not have happened. Thank you.